CW01162793

Why are we doing this again?

The first Terrible Parables book was hot garbage.

I just can't stop myself.

Once I get a dumb idea in my head, I'm going to run that idea into the ground.

As I said last time, any warped theology or accidental heresy is unintentional.

Here we go.

The kingdom of heaven is like a kid who asked to play a board game with her dad. After playing, the kid said, "One more game!" So they played again. After the second game, the kid said "Just one more time. Please?" The dad replied "Fine. One more game, but that's it."

But the pattern repeated, and they ended up playing seven games in a row.

The kingdom of heaven sneaks up on you like the common cold during the Covid pandemic. You spend all of your time fearing the Covid virus, and forget about the other viruses that are also out there, and then suddenly you're lying in bed binging The Bachelor and eating only saltine crackers for 2 days.

Sure, it's not Covid.

Still sucks though.

The kingdom of heaven is like a slice of pineapple that's placed on a hamburger patty on the grill. The pineapple slice slides off of the patty and into the grill. After all of the burgers are done being grilled, the GrillMaster removes the pineapple slice from inside the grill and throws it into a nearby bush, where it feeds a hungry squirrel.

The kingdom of heaven is like a Charleston Chew. It's not the most popular candy bar. Honestly, until this moment, you probably forgot that they existed.
But they do, and they're delicious.

The kingdom of heaven is like Liz Phair's self-titled album. It was unappreciated when it came out, and it certainly wasn't what people expected. A ton of people wrote off Liz Phair after that album dropped. They absolutely despised it.
But those people were wrong. That album rules.
Fight me.

(Okay, there's that one song that makes me really uncomfortable. I'm no prude, but that song's a little much for me. But other than that one song, great album.)

The kingdom of heaven is like a kid who saw his sister running a 5k and decided to join the race.

Without telling his parents.

The parents and their friends searched everywhere for him. The organizers of the race searched for him. The park ranger searched for him.

After a significant amount of time, a friend of the kid's parents saw him running and recognized him, so she ran alongside him all the way to the finish.

The kid was reunited with his parents, and the race organizers gave him a medal for finishing the race.

The kingdom of heaven is like Carly Rae Jepsen's album *Emotion*. The album came out without a ton of fanfare. Nobody really talked about it at first.

And like, I get it. The "Call Me Maybe" girl? Sure, that was a fine song, but the whole album was kinda meh. *Emotion* surely wouldn't be much better.

But it was. It's a freaking masterpiece.

Honestly, the fact that "Run Away With Me" wasn't as popular as "Call Me Maybe" is a crime. It's one of the best songs I've ever heard. The saxophone that kicks off that song is heavenly.

The kingdom of heaven is like that saxophone.

The kingdom of heaven is like the wrinkles on the face of a man in his late 30's. At first his baby face had no wrinkles, but as he progressed through his 30's, the amount of wrinkles grew larger.

The kingdom of heaven is like a high school track coach who organized the Pepsi Mile as a post-season event. Each person would chug a 12 oz Pepsi, then run a lap on the track. Chug another Pepsi, run another lap.

Four laps, five Pepsi's.

Sure, everyone vomited. Sure, parents didn't love the event. And sure, the mere sight of Pepsi caused every participant to gag for the following six months.

But the coach persisted, and it became a great memory for everyone involved.

The kingdom of heaven is like the cheerleading squad that watched the author of this book vomit directly in front of them after running the Pepsi Mile.

Their cheer practice was interrupted in the most horrible way possible, but they continued their practice regardless.

The kingdom of heaven is like this: Suppose a kid has approximately 72 billion Legos but loses the very specific one he needs. Does he not sweep the entire house looking for it? Does he not force his dad to go looking for it also? And when he finds it, he calls his neighbors to celebrate with him. "Rejoice with me! I have found my lost Lego!"

The kingdom of heaven is like a kid with a rock collection, but every rock is just an ordinary rock. There are no smooth, glittery, or shiny rocks in the collection. Only ordinary, jagged, gray rocks.

And yet, every dang time that kid goes outside, he finds a new rock for his rock collection.

The kid's parents consider getting rid of the rock collection, as it's taking over the kid's room. However, the rock collection is one of the kids' most prized possessions. Even more than the toys and books that his parents spent money on.

The kid loves and treasures his ordinary rocks.

The kingdom of heaven is like a kid who got to stay with her grandparents for the weekend. The snacks and junk food were neverending, and bedtime was more of a recommendation than a rule.

Will she be an absolute nightmare for her parents when she returns having eaten 12,305 cupcakes and only slept for 3 hours? Sure.

But that's in the future. And the future can wait.

The kingdom of heaven is mysterious, like a band who releases an NFT. What even is an NFT, and why is a band releasing one? Nobody knows.

Some crypto-bros with podcasts pretend to understand them, but those people are stupid and you really shouldn't listen to them.

The kingdom of heaven is like the first concert you're able to attend after the Covid vaccine is available.

The kingdom of heaven is like a spider whose web was destroyed by a hiker walking through it. The spider may be distraught, but immediately begins spinning a brand new web.

The kingdom of heaven is like a hiker that walks through a spider web. He screams and swats at the air for 5-10 seconds, but is ultimately content that the web has been entirely removed from his clothing.

The kingdom of heaven is like the hiker's friends who watch him walk through a spider web. They didn't go on this hike expecting a comedy show, but for 5-10 seconds, they get to watch their friend absolutely flip out for no reason. All of the friends experience an immense amount of joy (at the expense of their hiking buddy).

The kingdom of heaven is like one of the hiker's friends who runs into a different spider web later on in the hike. This friend now gets to entertain the original victim of the spider web with his own flailing, swatting, and screaming.

The kingdom of heaven is like a guy who went on a hike with his family and twisted his ankle a ways into the hike. He was in excruciating pain for the rest of the day, but ultimately made it back. And the rest of his family had a good time, so that's cool.

The kingdom of heaven is like a freshly vacuumed floor. For a very brief time, all of the dust particles are gone, and the carpet looks nice again.

The kingdom of heaven is like a Slurpee machine. When a child sees it, she begs her parents to buy her a Slurpee. When the parent says "no," she continues to ask unceasingly until she has that cup of sugary goodness in her hands.

The kingdom of heaven is like the ninth movie in a bad horror franchise. Somewhere around movie 4 or 5, you're furious that the series has "lost its way" and "will never be good again." But by movie 9, you've accepted the series for what it is: stupid fun. Watching it with friends is a joy.

The kingdom of heaven is like Paul Blart: Mall Cop. You don't hear many people talking about it these days, but it's still here. It never left. And it never will. You can still find it today in the DVD bargain bin at Walmart.

The kingdom of heaven is like an ostrich. My kid says that their eyes are bigger than their brains. That's a pretty cool fact.

The kingdom of heaven is like that fact. Pretty cool.

The kingdom of heaven is like a zebra. It looks like a horse, but cooler. And it can't be domesticated.

The kingdom of heaven is like chess boxing. Chess boxing is exactly what it sounds like. You play chess for three minutes, then you box for three minutes, then you play chess for three minutes, etc. You win by checkmate or knockout. It's the single most extreme sport I've ever heard of. How is this not on ESPN every week? How has Netflix not made a Queens Gambit/Rocky crossover movie about chess boxing? The people demand it.

The kingdom of heaven is like a coffee stain on a nice pair of dress pants. Sure, it looks unprofessional, but it's a part of you now. Accept it.

The kingdom of heaven is like terrible knock-knock jokes. They're awful. Objectively terrible. Like, really really bad. But kids like them, so they're gonna stick around.

Knock knock
Who's there
Shore
Shore who
Shore hope I never have to hear another knock knock joke again in my entire life.

The kingdom of heaven is like that one smooshed cupcake in the pack of twelve that you bought for a birthday party. Yeah, it's not as pretty as the others, but it will make its eater happy nonetheless.

Just make sure you give it to one of the adults, because if eleven kids get nice cupcakes and you give the twelfth kid a smooshed cupcake, that kid will cry.

The kingdom of heaven is like the stubbornness of someone who refuses to replace an electric razor, even though it hardly works anymore.

The kingdom of heaven is like racquetball. It's impossible to play, because the ball moves at approximately 40,000 miles an hour, and you know those goggles aren't gonna do a dang thing if the ball hits you in the face. But you keep playing anyway because "it's fun" and "exercise is good for you" and "you'll get the hang of it soon" and "it's really fun once you get it, I promise."

The kingdom of heaven is like a game of Monopoly. It goes on forever.

The kingdom of heaven is like the nine months of rain that we get each year in Portland. Sure, it triggers my depression something fierce. But it helps to keep us from experiencing wildfires in the summer.

I try and remind myself of this every March, but reminding myself doesn't do a dang thing.

Not a fan of constant rain.
Not. One. Bit.

The kingdom of heaven is like Pokemon. It started as this small little thing, and nobody could have possibly anticipated what a big deal it would become.

The kingdom of heaven is **not** like Pokemon, in the sense that Pokemon is basically about forcing animals to fight, and that's not cool.
The kingdom of heaven does not support or endorse animal fights.

The kingdom of heaven is like a rare Pokemon card. A person searches for their whole life to find it, and when they do, they treasure it.

The kingdom of heaven is NOT like the scalper who sells a Pokemon card for $5000. What the heck, dude? Why are you the way that you are? Who made you like this?

The kingdom of heaven is like a pair of tweezers to an ingrown hair.

The kingdom of heaven is like an ice pack to a 40-year-old lower back.

The kingdom of heaven is like putting in a fresh pair of contacts.

The kingdom of heaven is like the joy of receiving a notification on your phone that you've earned a free Big Mac.

The kingdom of heaven is like when you trip but catch yourself before you hit the ground, and save yourself a bloody and bruised face.

The kingdom of heaven is like when you trip and DON'T catch yourself, and your face gets bloody, bruised, and a bit mangled. Yeah, you hurt. You hurt a lot. You'd give anything to get rid of the pain.

But you also have a cool story to tell people at parties, and thats fun.

The kingdom of heaven is like the 90s album Jock Jams: Volume 1. You think it's going to be awful. The cover art is terrible. It's an album put out by ESPN. And *it's called Jock Jams.* This thing's gonna suck.

But then you put it in, and holy crap! 59 and a half minutes of bangers. You listen to it front to back, and you're amped up for the next five hours.

The kingdom of heaven is like the 90s album Pure Funk, for all of the same reasons.

It's perfect. Absolutely perfect.

The kingdom of heaven is like The Monster Mash. A bouncy novelty Halloween song with barely any singing; just Bobby Pickett talking about how a mad scientist's monster came up with a popular dance move.

It's stupid.

But I'm so happy anytime it comes on. As are you. As is everybody. Because it's perfect.

Tell me you don't sing "THEY DID THE MASH" when the chorus hits. Tell me with a straight face. You can't, because you totally do, because you love the song.

The kingdom of heaven is like the person who had the idea to buy old paintings from Goodwill and paint monsters onto them.

A Thomas Kinkade with a Godzilla-like monster in the background is hilarious.

The kingdom of heaven is like a guy wearing an ugly hat with a giant brim. Sure, he might look a little dumb, but after a full day in the sun, his face was never sunburned.

The kingdom of heaven is like dropping 3000 bouncy balls down a staircase. It's chaotic; it's colorful; it's beautiful. Cleaning it up is a pain, though.

The kingdom of heaven is like a singer who rewrote and re-recorded a song of theirs that had problematic lyrics.

The kingdom of heaven is like a mall Santa, who continues making kids happy throughout the day, even though 80% of them have cried in his lap, and 5% have peed on him.

The kingdom of heaven is like a parent who forgets to give tooth fairy money to their kid, but comes up with a convincing lie in the morning about how "The tooth fairy hit some traffic on the way to our house, but texted me and said she'll be here tonight instead."

Wait, are any kids reading this? Shoot. What I meant to say was: The kingdom of heaven is like the tooth fairy, who is definitely, absolutely, positively 100% real, and is not something your parents made up.

The kingdom of heaven is like somebody named Karen who has to endure the agony of having a name that's become synonymous with awful customers.

The kingdom of heaven is like a fruit fly. Their average lifespan is under two months, but they make the most of those two months.

By ticking off humans.

The kingdom of heaven is like a boss who emails information to their staff instead of forcing them into a boring and useless two hour meeting.

The kingdom of heaven is like employees who have to endure a useless two hour meeting that could have been an email.

The kingdom of heaven is like a giraffe fight. It's hilarious and brings so much joy to anyone watching.
Seriously, look up videos on YouTube. They fight with their necks. It's incredible.

The kingdom of heaven is like those flailing tube guys outside of used car lots. How it helps sell cars, I'll never know. But they're fun to watch.

The kingdom of heaven is like a person who rides the teacups at Disneyland, and endures the nausea they feel for the rest of the day.

The kingdom of heaven is like googly eyes. Anything to which they're affixed is automatically 20 times better.

Is it vandalism to put googly eyes on things in public or in stores? Possibly. But it's fun vandalism.

The kingdom of heaven is like fun vandalism.

The kingdom of heaven is like the satisfaction of watching creamer mix into a cup of coffee.

The kingdom of heaven is like getting a 1 in Wordle.
(Yes, I still play Wordle. And yes, I did get a 1 once. It was a glorious day.)

The kingdom of heaven is like a bench in the shade next to a playground. You're going to be on that bench for at least an hour. Shade is more valuable than gold for that hour.

The kingdom of heaven is like a ping-pong player who hits the ball exactly on the corner of her opponent's side. The opponent ignores it, thinking it's going to miss the table, and lives to regret that choice.

The kingdom of heaven is like a wedding DJ who is asked to play "Let the Bodies Hit the Floor" during the reception. He knows he will be hated by the vast majority of the attendees, but he plays it anyway.

It goes exactly as you'd think it would. Horribly.

The kingdom of heaven is like a kid who asks for the newest video game console for Christmas, but receives from his grandparents one of those bootleg consoles with illegal copies of terrible old video games loaded onto it. He smiles politely after opening it, in order to make his grandparents happy.

God bless those grandparents. They tried.

The kingdom of heaven is like a person riding an electric scooter safely, and not riding full speed directly toward people on the sidewalk.

The kingdom of heaven is like RC Cola. Pepsi and Coke get all of the accolades, but RC Cola is still there. Still fighting for any recognition at all.

It's hopeless, though.

Stop trying to make RC Cola happen.

It's not going to happen.

The kingdom of heaven is like Peeps Pepsi. It was obviously a terrible idea from the beginning, but the Pepsi company did it anyway. They took a big swing, and released a combination of the sugariest drink and the sugariest snack onto an unsuspecting public.

The kingdom of heaven is **not** like the person who decided to name it Peeps Pepsi instead of Peepsi.

You missed a golden opportunity, and you should be ashamed.

The kingdom of heaven is like a kid who listens to their parents and doesn't have to touch the stove to learn not to touch the stove.

The kingdom of heaven is like the bandits from Home Alone. They endured getting hit in the face with a crowbar, an iron, and a paint can, shot with a BB gun, getting burned in the head by a blowtorch, attacked by a swarm of pigeons, falling from a treehouse, and stepping on a nail, and they kept pursuing their goal.

Okay, their goal was to rob a house and kill Kevin in the process, so maybe the kingdom is not like the bandits from Home Alone.

The kingdom of heaven is like the writer of Home Alone, who somehow successfully turned what should have been a violent horror movie into a family classic.

Still violent. Still horrifying. But somehow family friendly.

The kingdom of heaven is like starting anywhere but the center in Tic-Tac-Toe. You're probably throwing the game, but showing great bravery in doing so.
You got moxie, kid.

The kingdom of heaven is like a team of people who enter a restaurant's "Eat the Entire 15 Pounds of Food and it's Free" contest and win.

Their stomachache was worth it.

The kingdom of heaven is like a kid who loses her favorite stuffed animal while on vacation. The parents go to the nearest toy store, and the store thankfully has the exact same stuffed animal in stock.

The parents buy it, and never, ever, ever, EVER tell the kid that the stuffed animal is a replacement. Ever.

The kingdom of heaven is like a kid that turns down the sound on his annoying toy so his parents can regain their sanity.

The kingdom of heaven is like a kid who blows a bunch of dandelion seeds onto his neighbor's lawn. His neighbor is proud of their perfectly green and nicely manicured lawn, and now they get to enjoy beautiful dandelions on the lawn as well! Hooray!

The kingdom of heaven is like someone who brings bags and cleans up after their dog when they take the dog on a walk.

The kingdom of heaven is like the people who ran spacejam.com, the website for the 90's movie Space Jam. Until recently, that website was still online, untouched. They preserved the domain for all these years, and never updated the site.
It looked terrible; wonderfully so.

When the second Space Jam movie was released, they updated the site, but still preserved the old site at spacejam.com/1996
It still looks terrible. Wonderfully so.

The kingdom of heaven is like a movie that you loved as a kid, and then watch as an adult and realize how terrible it is, but you still love it anyway because nostalgia is a powerful drug.

The kingdom of heaven is like a college class with an open book final exam.

The kingdom of heaven is like a college student who uses a weird font, bigger margins, and slightly wider spacing so they can write a shorter essay and still fill the required page count. Despite the cheating being completely obvious, their teacher doesn't lower their grade, merely giving the student a warning.

The kingdom of heaven is like the same student who has the gall to try the same thing on their next essay. Their teacher gives the student an F, but the student takes it in stride.

The kingdom of heaven is like the patience of the teacher when the same student tries the same deception YET AGAIN. It takes the teacher all of her strength to keep from screaming and swearing at the student.

The kingdom of heaven is like the person who makes sure every person's harness in the roller coaster is locked and secure.

The kingdom of heaven is like a boys cabin at camp that is actually clean and smells good.
(I'm stereotyping, but also not. I've been a camp counselor many times. Boys' cabins are gross.)

The kingdom of heaven is like the McRib, which continues to return to the McDonald's menu, no matter how many times it's been discontinued.

The kingdom of heaven is like that cool S that everyone learns to write in middle school.

The kingdom of heaven is like a person who listens to a terrible, horrible, no good, very bad cover version of a fantastic song. After listening and wanting to rip their ears off, they are reminded of how much they love the original version, and they play it immediately.

They never again mention the cover version.

The kingdom of heaven is like a person who flawlessly sings One Week, It's the End of the World as We Know It, We Didn't Start the Fire, and I Believe in a Thing Called Love at karaoke.

The kingdom of heaven is like a person who has to endure 3 intoxicated people from a bachelorette party absolutely butchering Baby Got Back at karaoke, but politely smiles and claps after they're done.

The kingdom of heaven is like someone who makes the toilet paper roll go over instead of under, just as God intended.

The kingdom of heaven is like a person who completes the Jumble, the Crossword, AND the Sudoku in the Sunday newspaper.

The kingdom of heaven is like a person who feels incredibly old when a middle school student asks them what a newspaper is, but they accept their age gracefully.

Then they take some Tums, pluck out some gray hairs, make an appointment with a chiropractor because their back always hurts, and complain about what's wrong with "the kids these days."

The kingdom of heaven is like Pete Best. He played in the most famous band of all time, yet nobody remembers him.

I know nothing about Pete Best. Do you know anything about Pete Best? I didn't think so.

But for a few years he was a Beatle, and nobody can take that away from him.

The kingdom of heaven is like a honey bee who stings a human, and in so doing, seals its own fate. The human cries, and the bee dies knowing that it fought the good fight and won.

The kingdom of heaven is like a dog and a cat who become friends. Sure, their parents may find it unnatural, but those parents don't understand that true friendship transcends species.

The kingdom of heaven is like a worship band that actually practices before the worship service, instead of winging it and then blaming Satan when it doesn't go well.

The kingdom of heaven is like those of you who are doing your best, even though life can be a constant struggle.
I'm proud of you.

I can't decide if I should thank you for reading this book, or apologize to you for wasting your time reading this book

Maybe both?

Thanks and I'm sorry

Milton Keynes UK
Ingram Content Group UK Ltd.
UKHW040255181024
449757UK00001B/34